# Park Life from Dinosaurs to Prairie Dogs

Samantha Bell

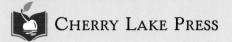

Published in the United States of America by Cherry Lake Publishing Group
Ann Arbor, Michigan
www.cherrylakepublishing.com

Reading Adviser: Beth Walker Gambro, MS, Ed., Reading Consultant, Yorkville, IL

Photo Credits: cover, title page: © Brita Seifert/Shutterstock; page 4: © Lorraine Logan/Shutterstock; page 5: © Dominic Laniewicz/Shutterstock; page 7: NPS Photo/Jim Peaco; page 8: NPS Photo/Jacob W. Frank; page 9: NPS Photo/Jacob W. Frank; page 11: NPS Photo/H. Kajitani; page 12: NPS Photo; page 13: © Carlos Gandiaga/ Shutterstock; page 14: © Anna Lisa Marten Miro/Shutterstock; page 17: © Ben McMurtray/Shutterstock; page 18: © B V Nickel/Shutterstock; page 21: NPS Photo; page 22: © Tom Reichner/Shutterstock; page 23: © Reimar/ Shutterstock; page 24: © Danita Delimont/Shutterstock; page 25: Unknown authorUnknown authorPhoto edited by User:PawełMM, Public domain, via Wikimedia Commons; page 27: © EpicStockMedia/Shutterstock; page 29: © Eric Carlander/Shutterstock; page 30: © Kryuchka Yaroslav/Shutterstock

**Cherry Lake Press** is an imprint of Cherry Lake Publishing Group.

Library of Congress Cataloging-in-Publication Data has been filed and is available at catalog.loc.gov.

Cherry Lake Publishing Group would like to acknowledge the work of the Partnership for 21st Century Learning, a Network of Battelle for Kids. Please visit http://www.battelleforkids.org/networks/p21 for more information.

Printed in the United States of America
Corporate Graphics

Note from publisher: Websites change regularly, and their future contents are outside of our control. Supervise children when conducting any recommended online searches for extended learning opportunities.

**Samantha Bell** was born and raised near Orlando, Florida. She grew up in a family of eight kids and all kinds of pets, including goats, chickens, cats, dogs, rabbits, horses, parakeets, hamsters, guinea pigs, a monkey, a raccoon, and a coatimundi. She now lives with her family in the foothills of the Blue Ridge Mountains, where she enjoys hiking, painting, and snuggling with their cats Pocket, Pebble, and Mr. Tree-Tree Triggers.

# CONTENTS

**Introduction | 5**

Chapter 1:
**Grizzlies, Wolves, and Pronghorns | 6**

Chapter 2:
**Foxes, Lizards, and Whales | 10**

Chapter 3:
**Black Bears, White-Tailed Deer, and Wild Turkeys | 16**

Chapter 4:
**Prairie Dogs, Ferrets, and Mosasaurs | 20**

Chapter 5:
**Sea Turtles, Coral Reefs, and Nurse Sharks | 26**

Plan Your Adventure | 30
Be an Advocate | 30
Learn More | 31
Glossary | 32
Index | 32

# Introduction

The national parks are full of interesting and amazing creatures. Visitors to the parks have opportunities to see these animals in their natural environments. The parks also play an important role in protecting these animals. Many of them are threatened or endangered. With the help of conservationists and the national parks, animals like the bison, island fox, and black-footed ferret are still here today.

# CHAPTER 1

# Grizzlies, Wolves, and Pronghorns

## Yellowstone National Park, Wyoming, Montana, and Idaho

Yellowstone National Park is famous for its wildlife. The park is home to 67 different species of mammals alone. One of the largest is the grizzly bear. Grizzly bears are a type of brown bear. Males can weigh up to 700 pounds (317.5 kilograms). Females can weigh up to 400 pounds (181 kg). Grizzlies can be aggressive, especially a mother bear with cubs. If park visitors see a grizzly bear, they should stay at least 100 yards (91 meters) away. Long ago, grizzly bears roamed large areas of the West. Today, they are only in a few locations. Approximately 150 grizzly bears live in Yellowstone National Park.

Male grizzly bears can weigh up to 700 pounds (317.5 kg).

Pronghorns have benefited from conservation programs. There are nearly 500,000 alive today.

Yellowstone is also home to the gray wolf. The northern range of the park is one of the best places in the world to see these wolves. The wolves travel together in groups called packs. They hunt for prey such as elk, deer, or bison. When wolves kill their prey, coyotes, bears, and birds will eat it, too. Wolves were living in Yellowstone when the park opened in 1872. But settlers moving westward used the land for their **livestock**. The wolves' habitat became smaller. They attacked the livestock, and then people killed the wolves. By the 1940s, there were no more packs in Yellowstone. **Conservationists** have worked hard to bring them back.

Another animal once threatened by **overhunting** is the pronghorn. These unusual animals look like antelope. But they are more closely related to giraffes. Pronghorns live in the grasslands of Yellowstone. They eat grasses, shrubs, and wildflowers. They are the fastest land mammal in North America, and the second-fastest in the world. They can sprint 45 to 50 miles (72 to 80 kilometers) per hour. When settlers first moved west, approximately 35 million pronghorns lived there. The herds were soon wiped out by hunters and ranchers. Because of conservation programs, nearly 500,000 pronghorns are alive today. Approximately 500 live in Yellowstone National Park.

# BRINGING BACK THE WOLVES

By the mid-1900s, wolves had been almost completely eliminated in the lower 48 states. But from 1995 to 1997, 41 wild wolves from Canada and northwest Montana were released in Yellowstone. Some of the wolves established territories outside the park. They are less protected than the others. But as of 2021, there are at least 95 wolves in Yellowstone.

# CHAPTER 2

# Foxes, Lizards, and Whales

## Channel Islands National Park, California

The Channel Islands are made up of eight islands off the coast of Santa Barbara, California. Five of the islands are part of the Channel Islands National Park. They are home to many rare and unusual species. Island foxes live on the three largest islands in the park. These foxes have similar markings to a gray fox. But they are about the size of a house cat. In the 1990s, the number of foxes greatly decreased. Golden eagles began breeding on the islands. They preyed on the foxes. Conservationists removed the eagles. They started a **captive breeding program** for the foxes. With their help, the number of island foxes has increased.

Island foxes live on the three largest islands in Channel Islands National Park.

Another rare animal in the park is the island night lizard. They are found only on the Channel Islands. These lizards are actually most active in the middle of the day. Unlike most reptiles, they give birth to live young. The young lizards grow slowly. Adults grow to be about 3 to 4 inches (7.6 to 10 centimeters) long. They can live up to 25 years. But when non-native animals were brought to the islands, the lizards began to disappear. Goats, pigs, and rabbits were changing the habitat. Feral cats were preying on the lizards. Once these animals were removed, the lizard population began to increase again.

Inspiration Point on Anacapa Island in the Channel Islands

Dolphins can be found around the Channel Islands throughout the year.

The water surrounding the park is full of wildlife, too. About one-third of the world's whale, dolphin, and porpoise species can be seen in the Channel Islands. Whale species include gray, blue, humpback, and pilot whales. Visitors to the park can enjoy whale watching all year long. They can spot gray whales from December through mid-March. Blue and humpback whales come by during the summer. Dolphins are around the islands throughout the year. Visitors can look for whales and dolphins from shore or from a boat. The visitor center has a tower with telescopes for whale watching, too.

# A VERY LARGE GATHERING

San Miguel Island is one of the Channel Islands. It is a favorite location of seals and sea lions. Each year, thousands come to the island to have their young. This includes about 70,000 California sea lions and 5,000 northern fur seals. Approximately 50,000 northern elephant seals and 1,100 harbor seals come, too. Sometimes rare Guadalupe fur seals and Steller sea lions also spend time on the island. Visitors can take a long hike to Point Bennett to see the seals. It is one of the best locations for viewing the animals.

# CHAPTER 3

# Black Bears, White-Tailed Deer, and Wild Turkeys

## Great Smoky Mountains National Park, Tennessee and North Carolina

Most of the Great Smoky Mountains National Park is covered by dense forest. During the winter, the leaves fall from many of the trees. This makes it easier to view wildlife in the park. One of the most well-known animals in the park is the American black bear. It is also the symbol of the Smoky Mountains. The park provides the largest protected bear habitat in the eastern United States. About 1,500 black bears live in the park.

American black bear cubs climb a tree in Great Smoky Mountains National Park.

Male white-tailed deer are called bucks. Bucks grow antlers. Their antlers fall off every year and regrow in the spring and summer.

The bears are not aggressive, and attacks are rare. But they are wild animals and can be unpredictable. It is illegal to get closer than 50 yards (46 m) to a black bear.

White-tailed deer also live throughout the park. They are most often seen in open fields. **Fawns** are born in June. Females usually have one to three fawns. They have reddish coats with white spots. This helps them stay safe from predators by blending in with the forest. Predators include bobcats, bears, and coyotes. The deer eat a variety of plants in the park. During the spring and summer, leaves and grasses are a nutritious food source. In the fall and winter, they eat more woody twigs and acorns.

The park is also home to North America's largest ground-dwelling bird, the wild turkey. These birds spend much of the year together in a flock. They have very good eyesight and are watchful for nearby predators. When European settlers first arrived, the turkeys were plentiful. But by the early 1900s, only a few were left. Overhunting and habitat destruction wiped out most of the birds. In the 1950s, biologists began capturing some of the survivors. They relocated them to their old habitats. Today, about 500 wild turkeys live in the Great Smoky Mountains National Park.

# HOME SWEET HOME

The Great Smoky Mountains National Park is also known as the Salamander Capital of the World. Salamanders are amphibians that live near or in water. Unlike reptiles, they do not have scales. Their skin is moist. The park is an ideal habitat for salamanders. The mountain forests are dense and shady. The park contains more than 700 miles (1,127 km) of streams. Thirty different species of salamanders can be found in the park.

# CHAPTER 4

# Prairie Dogs, Ferrets, and Mosasaurs

## Badlands National Park, South Dakota

Many kinds of animals live in Badlands National Park. Some have large populations. Others are among the most endangered species in North America. Prairie dogs live in burrows that they dig in the ground. Prairie dogs that are related dig burrows next to each other. They create large communities called towns. In the Badlands, hundreds of black-tailed prairie dogs live in Roberts Prairie Dog Town. They use calls to alert each other of predators. Eagles, hawks, and owls rely on prairie dogs as a food source.

Prairie dogs stand on their hind legs and let out a warning cry to other prairie dogs. Sometimes they do this to test their warning system. Sometimes there is a real threat.

Rattlesnakes often sun themselves on rocks, roadways, and paths.

So do foxes, coyotes, and rattlesnakes. Prairie dogs play another important role. Their burrows provide a habitat for approximately 200 animal and plant species.

Another animal that depends on prairie dogs is the black-footed ferret. Prairie dogs make up 90 percent of their diet. The ferrets live in abandoned prairie dog burrows. That way, they are close to their food source. The burrows also keep them safe from harsh weather and predators. These ferrets almost disappeared completely when people moving west wanted to farm the land.

The prairie dogs were often **exterminated**. Without their main food source, the ferrets began to die out. In 1980, they were declared extinct. Then in 1981, a small colony was discovered in Wyoming. Since then, captive breeding programs have helped bring them back. Today, there are about 120 black-footed ferrets in the park.

# BONES IN THE BADLANDS

Badlands National Park is also a good place to discover creatures that lived thousands of years ago. The park is known for its abundance of fossils. Some of the fossils are from mosasaurs. These giant marine reptiles had sharp teeth and long, powerful tails. Mosasaurs could be up to 50 feet (15 m) long. For some, their tails made up half of the length. If the Tyrannosaurus rex was the top predator on land, the mosasaur was the top predator of the ocean. It ate anything it could catch.

Due to conservation efforts, there are about 20,000 bison alive today. About 1,200 call the Badlands their home.

The number of bison dropped from 30 million to only 325 when settlers started hunting them. This photo of bison skulls was taken outside of a fertilizer plant near Detroit, Michigan.

Another animal that has made a comeback is the bison. Before settlers moved west, at least 30 million bison roamed the land. They were an important part of the culture of Indigenous peoples throughout the continent such as the Lakota. Indigenous peoples used every part of a bison to make food, clothes, blankets, knives, and fuel. But in the 1800s, White hunters began killing the bison for their hides. In 1884, there were only 325 wild bison left. Conservationists began working to protect them. Today, there are about 20,000 bison. Approximately 1,200 live in the Badlands.

# Sea Turtles, Coral Reefs, and Nurse Sharks

## Dry Tortugas National Park, Florida

The Dry Tortugas National Park includes 100 square miles (259 sq. km) of open water with seven small islands. The islands are mostly made of sand and coral. Spanish explorer Ponce de León named the islands Las Tortugas, which means "the turtles." Five species of sea turtles swim around the islands. Green and loggerhead sea turtles also nest on the beaches. These species are listed as threatened. All of the other sea turtle species are endangered. The name of the islands was eventually changed to Dry Tortugas. This change was to let sailors know that there was no freshwater on the islands.

Green sea turtles are listed as threatened. The five species of sea turtles living around the islands gave them their name: Las Tortugas.

The park is also home to about 30 species of coral. Corals are tiny organisms that live and grow connected to each other. The coral itself is clear. But they host billions of colorful microscopic algae. These give the coral their bright colors. They also provide corals with additional nutrients. The coral reefs are complex ecosystems. They provide habitats for many marine animals. These include fish, lobsters, sponges, sea stars, and anemones. Many visitors to the park go snorkeling or scuba diving. The clear waters provide them with some of the best underwater viewing in the country.

# TURTLE TRACKING

National Park Service scientists have been watching the sea turtles and their nests since 1980. Every day during nesting season, the scientists visit each island in the park. They look for turtle tracks on the beaches. They also search for mounds of sand. These are the turtle nests. The scientists record every nest. After 45 days, they check the nests for **hatchlings**. After about 60 days, they go back again to count the number of eggs. They record how many have hatched, how many have not, and how healthy the eggs are. They use this information to figure out the best ways to help the turtles.

There are about 30 different species of coral in Dry Tortugas National Park.

The coral reefs also make the ideal habitat for nurse sharks. These sharks are slow-moving. They usually live in tropical and subtropical water that's less than 40 feet (12 m) deep. Nurse sharks are normally **docile**. People can swim with the sharks, although they may attack if they are provoked. Park scientists study the sharks. The sharks use the area as a **breeding ground**. By tracking the sharks, scientists have found out that some return to the Dry Tortugas year after year.

# Activity

## Plan Your Adventure!

**Wildlife abounds in the national parks. From bears to dolphins to prehistoric predators, there are creatures to capture your attention. Think about the animals you would like to see. Then do a little research to find out where they live. You may even find them in more than one national park. Then look through the other books in this series to find more to explore.**

## Be an Advocate

Many of the animals mentioned in this book are threatened or endangered. Choose one of these animals and learn more about it. Ask an adult to help you find more information at the library or online. Then design a poster to help make others aware of the problem. First, draw the animal in the center of the poster. Then add facts, ideas, quotes, or other text that could encourage people to care and help.

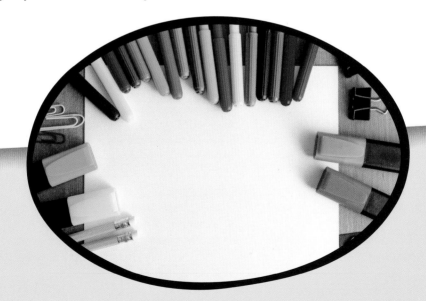

# Learn More

## Books

Figart, Francis. *A Search for Safe Passage.* Gatlinburg, TN: Great Smoky Mountains Association, 2021.

Hirsch, Andy. *History Comics: The American Bison: The Buffalo's Survival Tale.* New York, NY: First Second Books, 2021.

Musgrave, Ruth. *Dry Tortugas.* Vero Beach, FL: Rourke Educational Media, 2019.

Stuckey, Rachel. *Bringing Back the Black-Footed Ferret.* New York, NY: Crabtree Publishing, 2020.

## On the Web

With an adult, learn more online with these suggested searches.

"Ask a Ranger: Wild Animals." National Park Service.

"Bears – A Yellowstone Love Story." National Park Service.

"Day Hiking and Wildlife." Great Smoky Mountain National Park.

"Yellowstone National Park." San Diego Zoo Kids.

# Glossary

**breeding ground** (BREE-ding GROWND) a place where animals mate and produce young

**captive breeding program** (KAP-tiv BREE-ding PROH-grahm) the process of breeding animals in farms or zoos instead of their natural habitat to help increase the population

**conservationists** (kahn-suhr-VAY-shuhn-ists) people who help protect Earth's natural resources

**docile** (DAH-suhl) easy to manage or handle, not aggressive

**exterminated** (ik-STUHR-muh-nay-tuhd) to get rid of something by destroying it

**fawns** (FOHNZ) baby deer

**hatchlings** (HACH-lingz) baby animals that come forth from an egg

**livestock** (LYVE-stahk) horses, sheep, cows, or other animals raised on a farm or ranch

**overhunting** (oh-vuhr-HUHN-ting) any hunting activity that has negative impact on the population of a species

# Index

activities, 30

Badlands National Park, 20–25
bears, 6–7, 16–18
bison, 4, 24–25
black bears, 16–18
black-footed ferrets, 22–23

California, 10–15
Channel Islands National Park, 10–15
conservation, animals, 5, 6–9, 10–12, 16, 19, 23, 24–25, 28, 29
corals, 28–29

deer, 18–19
dolphins, 14, 15
Dry Tortugas National Park, 26–29

endangered species, 5, 22–23, 26–27, 30

ferrets, 22–23
Florida, 26–29
fossils, 23
foxes, 5, 10–11, 22

Great Smoky Mountains National Park, 16–19
grey wolves, 8, 9
grizzly bears, 6–7

hunting
by animals, 8, 10, 12, 20
of animals, 8–9, 19, 22–23, 25

Idaho, 6–9
island foxes, 5, 10–11

Lakota, 25
lizards, 12

marine life, 14–15, 23, 26–29
Montana, 6–9
mosasaurs, 23

national parks, 5, 6–9, 10–15, 16–19, 20–25, 26–29
North Carolina, 16–19
nurse sharks, 29

prairie dogs, 20–23
prehistoric reptiles, 23
pronghorns, 8, 9

rattlesnakes, 22
reptiles, 22, 23

salamanders, 19
San Miguel Island, 15
seals and sea lions, 15
sea turtles, 26, 27, 28
sharks, 29
Smoky Mountains, 16, 19
snakes, 22
South Dakota, 20–25

Tennessee, 16–19
turkeys, 19
turtles, 26, 27, 28

whales, 15
white-tailed deer, 18–19
wild turkeys, 19
wolves, 8, 9
Wyoming, 6–9, 23

Yellowstone National Park, 6–9